Grouping and classifying
Contents

Teachers' notes

Aims of this book

▲ To develop awareness of materials all around and identify their properties.
▲ To relate the properties of materials to their uses.
▲ To demonstrate the way different materials are used.
▲ To describe the differences between solids, liquids and gases.

Developing science skills

While it is not necessary to follow the activity sheets in order, they do provide progression. Pages 5 to 25 cover materials, properties and uses; pages 26 to 32 develop an understanding of solids, liquids and gases.

It is in 'doing' science that children learn best, but this also involves discussing, observing, predicting, measuring, recording, looking for patterns, classifying, explaining and asking questions which can lead to further investigations. Together, these aspects of learning will aid the teacher in monitoring the children's progress so that they build a valid framework for future development.

Safety precautions

The activities described in this book use everyday equipment and materials which are perfectly safe if used sensibly. Where extra care is needed, for example when glass or hot water is used, this is mentioned on the worksheet and emphasised in the teachers' notes. Remind children to wash their hands after handling materials.

Scientific background

Where necessary, information is provided to help with the understanding of scientific concepts and ideas covered in this book. It generally goes beyond the level of understanding expected of most children, but will give you the confidence to ask and answer questions and guide the children in their investigations.

Notes on individual activities

Page 5: Materials all around

Key idea: To identify and sort common materials.
Likely outcome: The materials identified will depend on the surroundings. Plastic and wood will probably prove to be the most commonly used materials.
Extension: Devise a game where materials are identified by touch only. Can all the materials be recognised and sorted when blindfolded?

Page 6: Marvellous metals

Key idea: Metals have special properties which determine their uses.
Scientific background: Although metals have common properties, there are often exceptions. Metals are hard, shiny, strong and often seem heavy; they normally feel cold, can be pulled and bent without easily breaking, can be beaten out into flat sheets and make a ringing noise when tapped; they conduct electricity and some demonstrate magnetic behaviour.

Likely outcome: Children are making decisions about why metal is used in different circumstances. Children may suggest alternative materials that are natural (stone, wood), or synthetic (plastic).
Extension: Put a few metal objects outside; pour water on them each day and observe what happens.

Page 7: Wonderful wood

Key idea: Wood is a versatile and attractive material to use.
Likely outcome: Wood is widely used (for example, in building). Outside it rots and splinters due to weathering. Many animals and plants will live and feed on wood.
Extension: Compare wood from different trees. Find out the different uses of each type of wood.

Page 8: Useful plastic

Key ideas: Plastic is a modern material, widely used in its many different forms because of its diverse properties, but difficult to recycle and dispose of.
Scientific background: There are many different types of plastic which are derived from oil. The different types, made from different arrangements of molecules, cannot be mixed. This makes recycling a problem (see p. 25 for an explanation of *recycling*). Sorting is necessary before the plastic can be recycled into pellet form and formed into new items; milk cartons can become plastic garden chairs. Children will need to be familiar with the terms transparent, waterproof and long-lasting before using the chart.
Likely outcome: Different types of plastic have different properties which make it a versatile and useful material. Because it is so durable it is difficult to get rid of and so recycling is important.
Safety note: Children should be supervised and wear protective gloves for the 'burying' activity.
Extension: See if you can find out some names given to different types of plastic.

Page 9: Fibres and fabrics

Key idea: There are many different fibres and fabrics which can be grouped and sorted.
Likely outcome: Synthetic fabrics are common and have unusual names. Sheep's fleece can easily be made into threads.
Note: Small pieces of raw fleece can be collected from fences and hedgerows or local spinners groups can often supply some. Advise children to wash their hands after handling fleece.
Extension: Find out how silk and linen are produced.

Page 10: Testing materials for hardness

Key ideas: Some materials are harder than others. A scratch test can determine hardness. Tools need to be made of a harder material than that on which they are working.
Scientific background: In 1812, a German, Friedrich Mohs, devised a scale of hardness which scientists still use today. Materials at 1 on the scale

are the softest. Diamond is the hardest at 15. Any new material can easily be positioned on the scale since harder ones scratch softer ones.
Likely outcome: Stone and metal will be found to be harder than plastic or wood.
Safety note: Children should adopt a safe method of working when using sharp objects. Materials being scratched should be held in a vice or held firmly to a desk by a G-clamp.
Extension: Investigate the hardness of different play surfaces, such as grass, tarmac, bark chippings, concrete. Which do the children think is the safest?

Page 11: Examining materials for strength

Key ideas: One type of material can vary in strength. Strong materials will resist forces and will support heavy loads.
Scientific background: Technical achievements are limited by the weaknesses of materials. Materials with the greatest strength are needed for constructing buildings, bridges and planes.
Likely outcome: Although it would be difficult for children to test the strength of one material against another, they can make decisions based on their experiences of the strengths of common materials. Drinks cans and aluminium foil are examples of metal losing some of its strength through thinness.
Extension: Look for examples of where strength is important for securing purposes such as anchor chains.

Page 12: Flexible materials

Key idea: Squashing and stretching are tests for flexibility.
Scientific background: A material which is completely flexible will return to its original shape. Some materials are only flexible due to their thinness.
Likely outcome: Materials demonstrate different degrees of flexibility. Flexibility is important where wrapping, covering or stretching is required. Flexible items include elastic bands, wire, string, foil, springs.

Page 13: Magnetic materials

Key idea: Only certain metals, and no non-metals, demonstrate magnetic behaviour.
Likely outcome: Some metals are pulled towards a magnet. Sometimes the attraction is strong, at other times weak. Children may get variable results with different aged items of metal. This is because older metal can often lose some of its magnetic attraction.
Safety note: Children must take care when handling sharp objects.

Page 14: Testing metals for magnetic behaviour

Key idea: Only cobalt, nickel and metals containing iron demonstrate magnetic behaviour.
Scientific background: Steel contains iron (although some stainless steel items do not show magnetic attraction).
Likely outcome: Many metals are not magnetic. Magnets can be used to sort metals.

Safety note: Activities involving iron filings need to be supervised. Please note that some LEAs have banned the use of iron filings in schools.
Extension: Look for examples where magnetic attraction is useful such as magnetic door catches.

Page 15: Materials and water

Key idea: Materials react differently when in contact with water.
Scientific background: Materials which are more dense than water will sink. Materials with air spaces will absorb water; as the water replaces the air, bubbles can be seen rising to the surface.
Likely outcome: Some materials sink, others float on or below the surface of the water. Those which absorb water become heavier.

Page 16: Travelling heat

Key ideas: Heat moves through materials from a warmer to a cooler area. Some materials allow heat to pass through them more quickly than others.
Scientific background: If a material is a good conductor of heat, the molecules of which it is made up vibrate vigorously as they become heated and heat is passed from one to the next very quickly. In a bad conductor (good insulator) of heat, the molecules only vibrate a little and do not pass on the heat.
Likely outcome: Metals are good conductors of heat. Cork and polystyrene are good insulators.
Extension: Find out the importance of choosing the best insulating materials when building a house.

Page 17: Keeping cool, staying warm

Key idea: Good thermal insulators can be used for keeping heat out as well as in.
Likely outcome: The ice cube which remains unwrapped will melt more quickly than those which have been thermally insulated; the tea cosy will help the liquid to retain its heat longer.
Safety note: The test using hot water must be organised safely by the teacher.
Extension: Find more examples of thermal insulation such as a cool box. Which types of clothing would you choose to stop heat escaping from your body. Find out how polar bears, seals and seagulls keep themselves warm.

Page 18: Materials conducting electricity

Key idea: Metals are good conductors of electricity; other materials resist the flow of electricity.
Likely outcome: The bulb will show most brightness when metal objects are used to bridge the gap; other materials will show degrees of resistance to the flow of electricity.
Extension: Find examples of the need for electrical insulators where it is vitally important that electricity should not be conducted through a material.

Page 19: Wear and tear

Key ideas: Some materials are more durable than others and are chosen for a purpose according to how they will stand up to the weather and regular use.
Likely outcome: The natural materials, wood, paper and fabric are most easily affected by methods of wearing; rubber and stone are less affected; metal, glass and plastic are the most durable.
Extension: Investigate further the durability of materials. A test could be rubbing with sandpaper.

Page 20: Boat-building

Key ideas: Many materials can be used to make a floating structure. Shape and stability are important.
Likely outcome: Plasticine, clay, aluminium foil, wood and paper boats can be constructed. Polythene can be used, but lids and cartons will need to be adapted for other types of plastic. Cargo on boats must be evenly spread to avoid disasters.
Extension: Research the past construction of boats.

Page 21: Materials for packaging

Key ideas: Many materials are suitable for packaging, depending on the object which needs to be wrapped. Some materials are specially designed to protect.
Likely outcome: Through discussion, decisions can be made about the suitability and effectiveness of materials for packaging.
Extension: Make a box to hold a favourite toy.

Page 22: What we can do with natural materials

Key idea: Natural or raw materials are changed into useful everyday items. Oil (and other materials) is changed by chemical processes to produce synthetic products.
Likely outcome: sheep's fleece → ball of wool → jumper; metal ore → metal ingot → nut and bolt; rocks → paving slabs → path.
Extension: Find out how sand is used to make glass, and how oil is used to make plastic.

Page 23: Using the best materials for the job

Key idea: The properties of a material determine its use.
Likely outcome: Individual decision-making based on an understanding of the properties of materials.

Page 24: Using the Earth's materials

Key ideas: Resources are diminishing and with time some materials will become harder to find. Others are renewable and, with careful management, their production could be sufficient for our needs.
Scientific background: Oil and metal ores are limited in their supply. Hardwood trees, which produce wood and rubber, are disappearing faster than new trees can grow. Softwood trees grow more quickly and could give a sustainable supply.
Likely outcome: Encourage children to discuss their ideas so they feel they can do something about the way materials are used. The use of hardwoods should be avoided (red), plastic, metal, natural fabrics, and paper should be used carefully (amber), and

although seemingly plentiful, softwood and glass should be used wisely (green). All suggestions should be respected.
Extension: Collect examples of the unnecessary use of materials, as in packaging. Make a board game which demonstrates the way in which the Earth's materials are used.

Page 25: What a waste!

Key ideas: Disposing of used materials is causing problems; recycling is a possibility with some materials.
Likely outcome: Each item will correspond to one recycling container. A – items of clothing, curtains; B – newspapers, comics and magazines; C – jars, bottles (mention what they contained); D – aluminium cans (mention what they contained).
Extension: Invite the local recycling officer to talk to the children.

Page 26: Solids, liquids and gases

Key idea: Materials can be identified and grouped according to whether they are solids, liquids or gases.
Scientific background: The molecules of solid materials are tightly packed. They are attracted to each other by strong forces and do not move about although they do vibrate. The molecules of a liquid are less strongly attracted and can slide over each other. The molecules of a gas move freely and in a random fashion.
Likely outcome: Solids – newspaper, shoe, brick; liquids – milk, engine oil, raindrops; gases – person's breath, car exhaust fumes, air inside a balloon.
The list of gases will be the most difficult to complete.
Extension: Prepare a large collage of cut-out pictures showing solids, liquids and gases.

Page 27: Looking at liquids

Key ideas: Liquids take the shape of the container they are in, and always find the lowest level possible.
Scientific background: A liquid has no fixed shape and because of the behaviour of its molecules, will move unless it is contained; due to the force of gravity, liquids move to the lowest level they can find.
Likely outcome: The coloured water takes on the interesting shapes of the containers and will change as the container is tilted.

Page 28: Moving liquids

Key ideas: Liquids behave differently from solids and gases; they drip and flow downwards.
Scientific background: The molecules of liquids cling together to form drops; drops form at different rates depending on the viscosity ('stickiness') of the liquid. Viscosity affects the rate at which liquids flow.
Likely outcome: Sticky liquids will form drops quite slowly which makes them easier to observe. The less sticky the liquid, the quicker it will reach the bottom of the slope.
Extension: Find out about flowing lava.

Page 29: Looking at gases

Key idea: Gases are difficult to observe, but their presence can often be detected by looking for clues.
Likely outcome: The bubbles of air pumped through the water in the fish tank provide oxygen for the fish; tanks supply the diver with oxygen while he is underwater; washing on the line is moved by the air (wind) as it is dried; hot air causes the balloon to rise.
Extension: Use the spiral snake to detect rising air around school.

Page 30: Making and collecting gases

Key ideas: A gas can be made by mixing materials; it is possible to collect a gas if you know it is there. It might be necessary to test the amounts of materials required which will vary according to the size of the bottle used.
Likely outcome: The reaction between bicarbonate of soda and vinegar is immediate; children can see, feel and hear the gas (carbon dioxide) as it escapes from the bottle into the atmosphere. The balloon will expand as the gas is collected. Names of gases may include oxygen, natural gas, carbon dioxide, nitrogen, CFCs, possibly carbon monoxide (car exhaust fumes), helium (some balloons), methane (decaying rubbish).
Safety note: Only plastic bottles should be used when mixing substances that react together.
Extension: Try the test again but stand the bottle in warm water. The gas will expand due to the heat and the balloon will inflate more.

Page 31: Comparing solids, liquids and gases

Key idea: There are differences and some similarities between solids, liquids and gases.
Likely outcome: A solid keeps its own shape, can sometimes be used for building and is usually easy to handle. A liquid flows downhill, flows easily through a pipe, drips, has no definite shape and takes the shape of the container it is in. A gas flows easily through a pipe, spreads out in all directions, has no definite shape and can be squashed into a smaller volume. Containers: solids – schoolbag, jar, cupboard, box; liquids – jar, bottle, hosepipe, straw, flask; gases – oxygen cylinder, balloon, pair of lungs.
Extension: Change ice to water and steam (carefully).

Page 32: Identifying solids, liquids and gases

Key idea: Solids, liquids and gases are all around us.
Likely outcome: 1 (planet Earth) solid – land; liquid – seas; gas – atmosphere. 2 (person) solid – skin, bones; liquid – blood, urine; gas – oxygen, carbon dioxide. 3 (tractor) solid – metal body, tyres; liquid – diesel, oil; gas – air in tyres, exhaust fumes. 4 (drink) solid – bottle; liquid – drink; gas – bubbles of carbon dioxide.

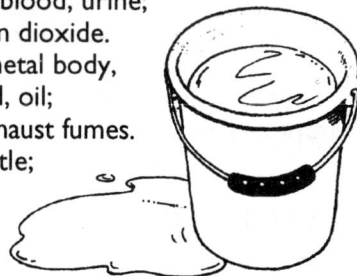

Materials all around

You will need: a pencil; a clipboard.
If you look around, you will see many different materials being used.

▲ Do three surveys. Look for things made of plastic, rock, metal, wood, fabric, paper, rubber and glass. Write their names in the table.

Materials	Survey 1 — Things I can touch without leaving my seat	Survey 2 — Things I can find around the classroom	Survey 3 — Things I can see when standing in the playground
plastic			
rock			
metal			
wood			
fabric			
paper			
rubber			
glass			

▲ Which materials seem to be the most common?
▲ Which category of material was the most difficult to find?
▲ Make a collection of each type of material. Display and label your collections.

Marvellous metals

You will need: wax crayons; pencils; paper.

▲ Collect as many of these metal objects as you can.
Decide why metal was used to make each object.
Could it have been made of any other material?

nail	key	piece of wire
paperclip	aluminium dish	1kg weight
drinks can	silver necklace	scissors
coin	bell	spoon

Metal object	Why metal was used	What other material could be used?
nail	It's strong and can be made sharp	none

▲ Make a list of all the things you have found out about metals.
Metals can be moulded into detailed shapes and patterns.
▲ Use pencils and crayons to make rubbings of metal objects
such as coins or keys. Use these to make a decorative collage.

Wonderful wood

You will need: a hand lens; pencils;
wax crayons; paper.

▲ Make a collection of pieces of wood and
objects made of wood. Use a hand lens to
examine each one. Write down everything
you notice about the appearance, pattern
and texture of wood.
▲ You will find wood is used for all kinds
of purposes. Can you find examples where
wood is important in these situations?

in building houses   **for sports equipment**
in art and craft activities   **in your bedroom**
for kitchen equipment   **for a method of transport**

▲ Record your ideas in the table.

Situation	Where wood is used	Why wood is used
Building houses		
Kitchen equipment		
Art and craft activities		
Transport		
Sports equipment		
Bedroom		

▲ Wood and weather: look around and
find out what happens to wood outside.
Examine dead branches and old doors and
window frames. Write down your
observations. Do some sketches.

You will have found different patterns
and textures in wood.
▲ Use pencils and crayons to make
rubbings and create a decorative collage.

Useful plastic

You will need: a collection of plastic items; some of
the same items in different materials; a pencil; paper.

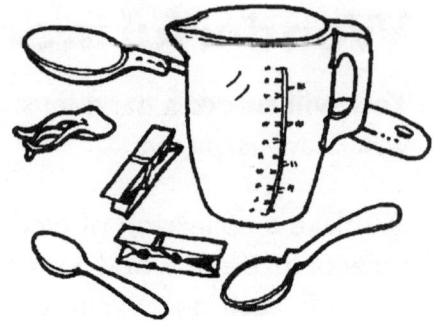

There are about 30 different types of plastic in general use.
▲ Collect ten plastic items that you use every day.
Examine them carefully and tick their properties in this table.

Name of item	thin	firm	transparent	can be folded	light in weight	waterproof	breakable	long-lasting

▲ Now find two items, one made of plastic
and the other made of a different material,
which both have the same use, like the
examples below.

plastic and wooden clothes pegs
plastic and metal spoons
plastic and glass jugs

▲ Compare the two items, writing down
the good points and bad points about each.

Getting rid of plastic can be difficult.
Rubbish is often buried.
▲ Bury some different types of plastic in the
ground together with some pieces of paper and
wood. Examine them every week and record
what happens to them.

Fibres and fabrics

You will need: a hand lens; a handful of sheep's fleece; a selection of fibres and fabrics; scissors; sticky tape; pieces of card; a pencil.

Fibres are threads that are put together to make a fabric which we call cloth. There are natural fibres, such as wool and silk from animals, and cotton and linen from plants; and synthetic fibres, such as nylon and polyester which are made using oil.

▲ Look at the labels on your clothes to find out what they are made of. Make a chart like this:

Clothing	Names of fibres	Natural or synthetic
T. shirt	cotton	natural

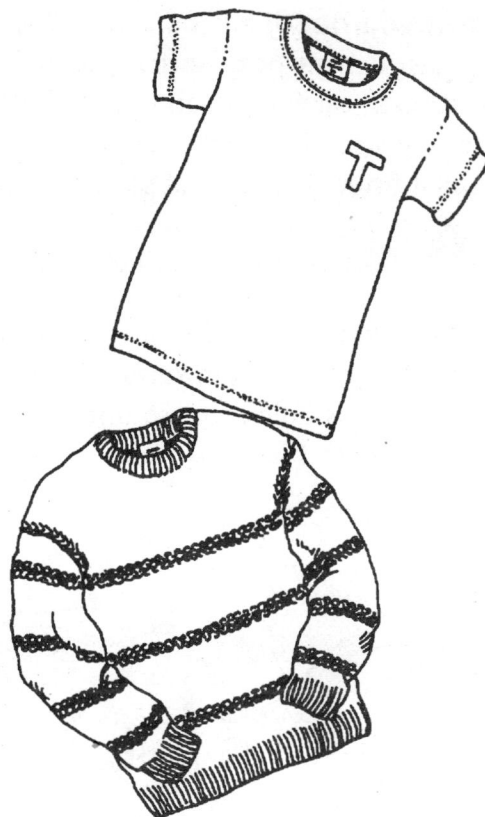

▲ Look closely at the fibres in sheep's fleece. Try twisting some with your fingers to make a thread.

Always wash your hands after touching fleece. Fibres are made into fabrics by weaving or knitting.
▲ Examine both sides of some fabrics with a hand lens. Try to draw and describe what you see. Can you tell whether they are woven or knitted? Sort the fabrics into these two groups. Label them and fasten small pieces on to cards.
▲ Try some weaving and knitting of your own.

Testing materials for hardness

You will need: a hand lens; objects to scratch such as a plastic plant pot, a brick, a pebble, pieces of wood, a rubber, cardboard, an old glass jar, an aluminium can; tools to scratch with such as a *used* matchstick (wood), a nail (metal), a strip of plastic, a sharp stone; a pencil.

⚠️ Take care when using sharp tools and glass objects.

When you want to know if something is hard or soft, you usually press the surface with your fingers.
▲ Use this quick test to find five hard objects and five soft objects. Make two lists.

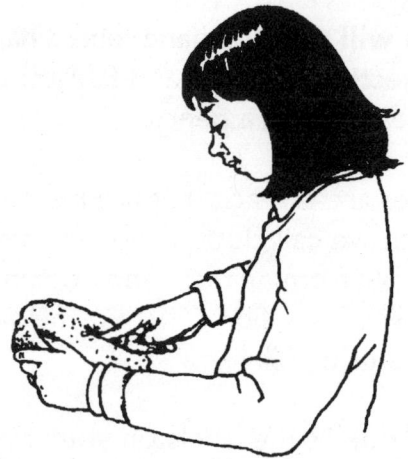

Scientists use a scratch test to see how hard a material is. If one material can scratch another, then it is harder. A scratch is a mark that cannot be rubbed away.
▲ Carefully scratch some objects with the tools you have collected. Each time, examine the scratch with a hand lens. Put ticks in the chart to show which tools left scratch marks.

Objects to scratch	Tools to scratch with			
	Wood	**Metal**	**Plastic**	**Stone**

The material which scratches the most other materials is the hardest.

▲ Can you put the materials in order of hardness?

Tools must be harder than the material on which they are used.

▲ Make a list of tools which are used for cutting paper, wood, plastic and metal.

Examining materials for strength

You will need: different types of paper;
a collection of items made from different
materials; a pencil; reference books.

One type of material can have varying strengths.
▲ Test different types of paper and record
your results.

Name of type of paper	Will it bend or fold?	Will it tear?	Will it stay firm when squashed or pulled?	Do you think it is strong? Use a scale of 1–10 (1 = weakest)

A material which is strong will not break
easily. It can support heavy loads.
▲ Look around and use books to find
examples of where strength is important in
buildings, machinery and transport. Make
drawings and label the materials used.

▲ When metal is made into thin sheets it is
not so strong. Can you think of examples?

▲ Collect these items and decide how
strong they are using a scale of 1–10 as above.

a piece of wood   **a sheet of paper**
a glass jar   **a pebble**
a rubber   **a piece of fabric**
something plastic   **a metal object**

Flexible materials

You will need: a collection of things
which are flexible; a hand lens; a pencil.

Materials which are flexible can be squashed,
squeezed, stretched, bent, folded, twisted
or wrapped around things. Anything which
is really flexible will always return to its
original shape.

▲ Examine a piece of sponge. Squeeze and
bend it. Look closely at its texture with a
hand lens.

▲ Make a list of things you have discovered
which are flexible.

▲ Sort your flexible things into groups
according to what material they are made of.

The opposite of flexible is firm or rigid.

Sometimes we need materials to be flexible.

Sometimes we need materials to be rigid.

▲ Make a list of examples of when we
need materials to be flexible.

▲ Make a list of examples of when we
need materials to be rigid.

Magnetic materials

You will need: a magnet; a collection of small items of different materials such as a pencil, a crayon, a coin, a plastic cube, a small stone, a piece of newspaper, a sock, a rubber, a glass jar, a paperclip; a pair of scissors; a pencil.

⚠ **Take care:** Magnets must be handled carefully. If they are dropped they can lose their magnetism. Magnets must be kept away from watches and electronic equipment.

Some materials are attracted to a magnet. Others are not affected by a magnet at all.
▲ Use a magnet to discover which things are attracted. Find out what material they are made of.
▲ Record your results.

These are different shapes of magnets:

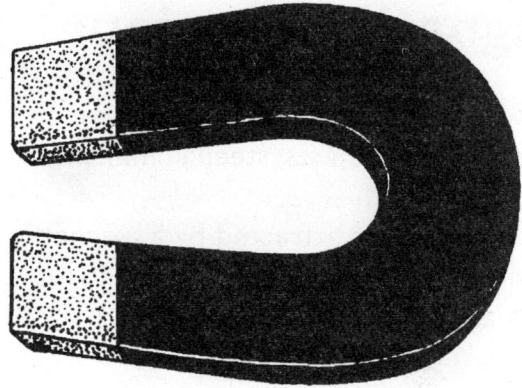

horseshoe magnet

bar magnet

Item you are testing	What material is it made of?	Was there an attraction? Was it strong or weak?

▲ Mix together a handful of paperclips and a handful of plastic counters. Find out if it is quicker to separate them by hand or using a magnet.

▲ Name _____

Testing metals for magnetic behaviour

You will need: a magnet; a collection of different metal objects; steel/aluminium cans.

Not all metals are attracted by a magnet.
▲ Find as many objects made of different metals as you can. Test them with a magnet.

piece of lead

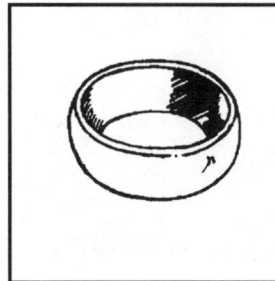
gold ring

silver necklace

aluminium foil

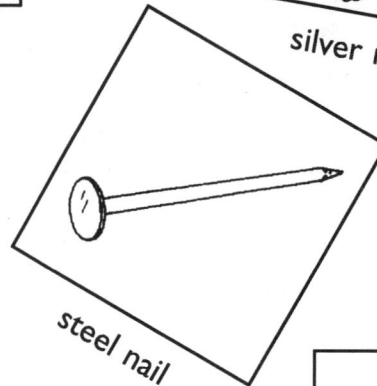
steel nail

copper wire

iron filings

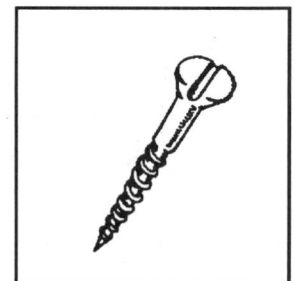
brass screw

▲ Sort your objects into two groups:
1 metals which show magnetic behaviour
2 metals which do not show magnetic behaviour.

Only cobalt, nickel and metals containing iron are attracted by a magnet.
▲ Use your magnet as an iron-finder. Make a list of objects you have found to contain iron.
▲ Collect drinks cans for recycling. Use a magnet to sort the cans according to whether they are steel (contains iron) or aluminium (contains no iron). Test the ends of the cans as well as the sides.

Materials and water

You will need: a large bowl or plastic tank to hold water; a bucket; objects to test; a pencil.

Some materials float, others sink.
▲ Test different objects to see whether they float or sink.
Try some of the items below.

a pencil   **a pebble**   **a cork**   **a lid**
a sponge   **an empty box** **a paperclip** **a rubber ball**

▲ Draw their position on the diagram.

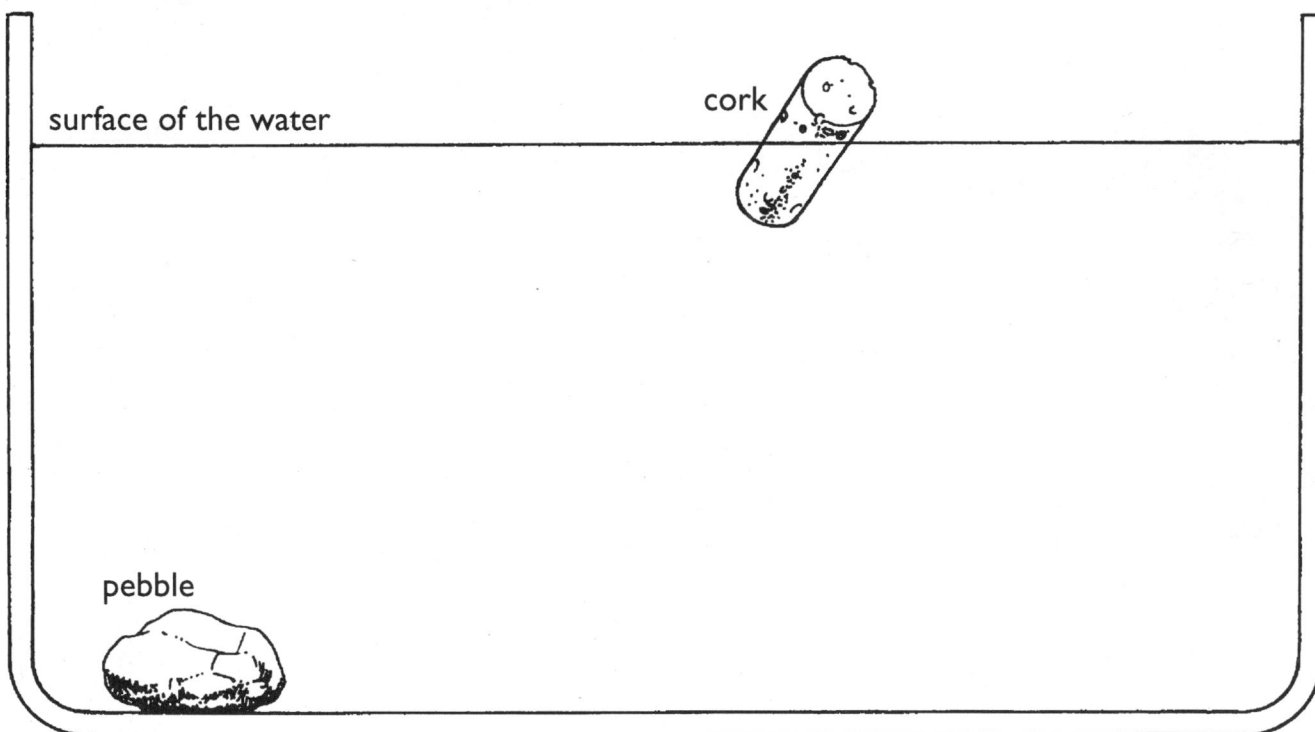

surface of the water   cork

pebble

▲ Sort the above objects into three groups:
1 things which float on the surface of the water
2 things which float beneath the surface of
the water
3 things which sink

Some materials soak up water.
▲ Which of these objects do you think will
soak up water?

a piece of paper   **a piece of fabric**
a sponge   **a metal spoon**
a plastic cube   **a piece of candle wax**
a brick

▲ Put them in a bucket of water for ten
minutes. How will you know if they have
soaked up any water?
▲ Sort the objects into two groups:
1 things which
soaked up water
2 things which are
waterproof

Travelling heat

You will need: a pencil; a collection of objects to test; supervised access to a hot radiator or sunny window sill; a freezer.

▲ Collect these objects for the tests.

a piece of card   something plastic
a cork   a metal object
a piece of fabric   a piece of
something wooden   polystyrene

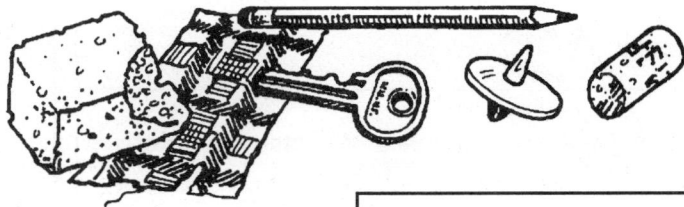

Heat is always trying to escape. It travels from hot spots to colder areas. Heat can travel through some materials more quickly than others.

▲ Find out which materials heat can travel through quickly. Use the chart to write down your results.

1 First, feel each object and decide whether it is hot, warm, cool or cold.
2 Put the objects in a warm place such as on a radiator or a sunny window sill.
3 After ten minutes, touch each object carefully and decide if there is any change.
4 Put the same objects in a freezer for ten minutes.
5 Quickly decide how they feel.

Name of object	How it felt			✗ ✓
	before the test	after being in a hot place	after being in a freezer	

▲ Put a tick next to the objects which quickly changed their temperatures.
▲ Put a cross next to the objects which hardly changed.

✓ These materials let heat pass through them easily. They are good conductors of heat.	✗ These materials did not let heat pass through them easily. They are good insulators of heat.

Keeping cool, staying warm

You will need: ice cubes; pieces of aluminium foil, newspaper, fabric, writing paper, cling-film; six small containers; tea cosy or something similar; hot water; two other containers.

⚠️ Take care when using hot liquids.

We often try to stop heat moving about. Sometimes we use materials to keep heat in, sometimes to keep heat out. The materials we choose are good *thermal insulators*.

▲ Find out which materials can stop heat reaching ice and melting it.

1 Quickly wrap each ice cube in a different material. You could use newspaper, writing paper, cling-film, aluminium foil and fabric.

2 Put each wrapped cube in its own container.

3 Put an unwrapped cube in a container too.

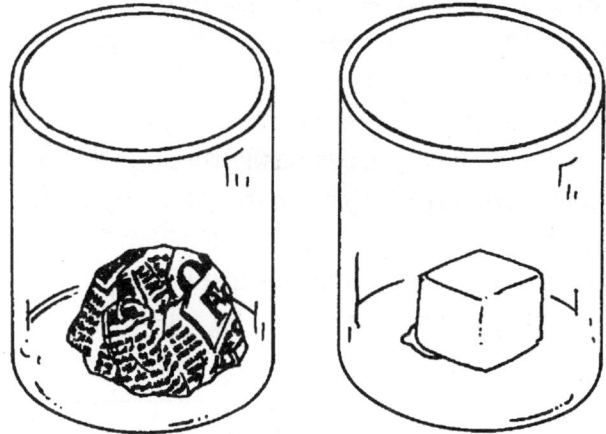

▲ Which ice cube was the first to melt?
▲ Which ice cube was the last to melt?
▲ Which material was the best at keeping the heat away from the ice – therefore the best thermal insulator?

▲ Does a tea cosy really work?

1 Ask an adult to fill two identical containers with hot water.

2 Carefully place a tea cosy, a woolly hat or a piece of fabric over one container.

3 Leave the containers for 15 minutes.

4 Very carefully feel the sides of the containers.

▲ Is there any difference in temperature?

Materials conducting electricity

You will need: equipment to make a circuit: a battery, covered wire, a bulb and bulb holder; wire cutters; two crocodile clips; materials to test; a pencil and crayons.

When electricity passes easily through a material, we say that the material is a good *conductor of electricity*.

▲ Find out which materials are useful for conducting electricity.

battery

bulb in holder

a circuit

wire

crocodile clips

Material	Did the bulb light up?	

1 First make a circuit, leaving a gap in the wire which can be joined by two crocodile clips as shown.
2 Separate the crocodile clips and bridge the gap with as many different materials as possible.
3 Record your results on this chart.
4 Colour the bulbs using the colour code below.

Colour code

Brightly lit bulb = orange

Dimly lit bulb = yellow

Unlit bulb = blank

Below are some materials to test.

aluminium foil
a stone
a key
a pencil
a piece of plastic
a chain of paperclips
a coin
a piece of card
a plastic ruler

▲ Try some materials of your own.

▲ Which materials are good at conducting electricity?
▲ Which materials will not conduct electricity at all?

Wear and tear

You will need: a pencil; a clipboard; a hand lens.

Most materials gradually wear away. They can be affected by people and animals using them, by plants growing on them and by the weather.

▲ Search for signs of wear and tear. Look around the inside and outside of the school.

▲ Record your findings on the chart.

Signs of wearing	Location	Possible reasons

▲ Choose words from the box to show what can happen to these materials.

wood _____

fabric _____

paper _____

rubber _____

plastic _____

metal _____

glass _____

stone _____

rots
tears
breaks
wears away
rusts/corrodes
shrivels
crumbles
can be eaten by
small creatures

Boat-building

You will need: a pencil; different materials for making boats such as paper and card, aluminium foil, Plasticine, modelling clay, wood, a piece of polythene, or any other materials you can think of; paperclips, counters or marbles; a large bowl or tank of water.

▲ Make three boats, each one out of a different material. Describe and test each one in a large bowl or tank of water.

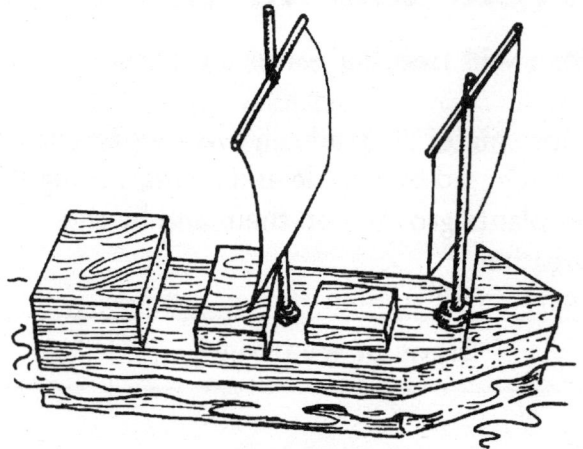

Draw your boat and give it a name	What material is it made of?	Make comments on the success and usefulness of your boat
1		
2		
3		

▲ Plan an investigation to see how successful your boats are at carrying cargo. You could use paperclips, counters or marbles.

▲ If you were building a people-carrying boat, which material would you use? Explain why.

Materials for packaging

You will need: a pencil; a collection of packaging materials; string; ribbon; sticky tape; glue; scissors.

Many objects need to be packed securely and safely.
▲ Collect some materials that could be used for packaging.
▲ Try and decide which are the best materials for packing these objects.

something quite small like a rubber
something larger like a book
something even bigger like a plastic (or glass) bowl or bucket

(You must also think how to fasten your parcels.)

▲ Record your ideas on this table.

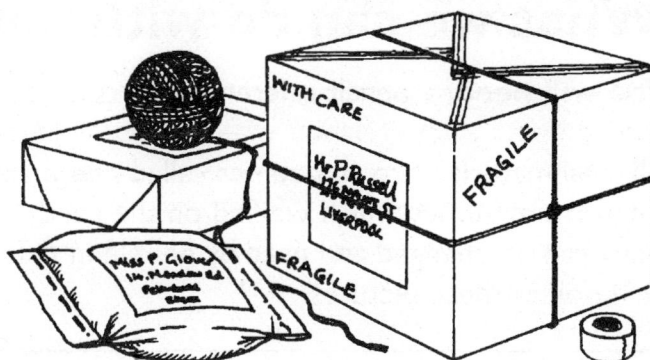

Packaging materials:

different types of paper	aluminium foil
polystyrene chips	cardboard
corrugated card	wallpaper
bubble wrap	newspaper
polythene	fabric
cling-film	card

Object	Packaging material	Why it is suitable

▲ How many different materials can be used for making boxes?
▲ Examine and sketch a box of each material. How are the pieces fastened together?

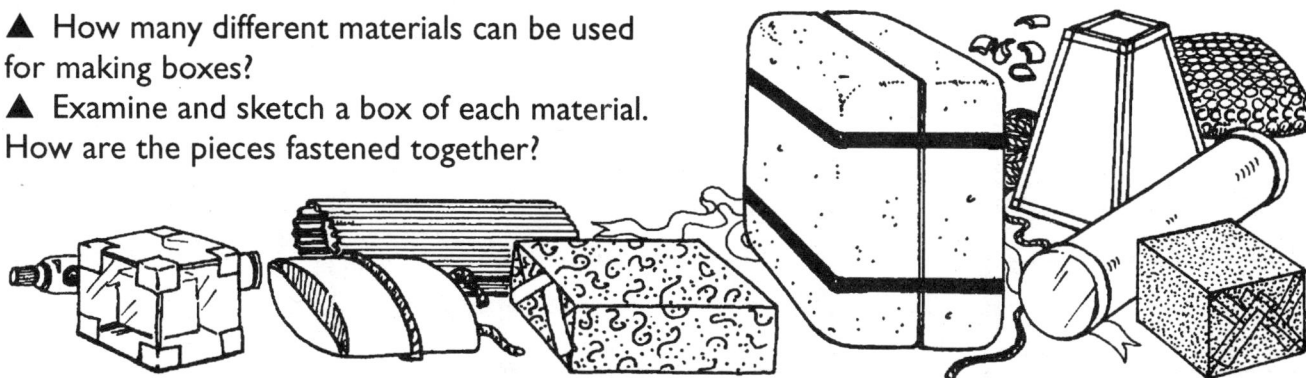

What we can do with natural materials

You will need: a pencil; reference books.

Natural materials are sometimes called raw materials.
They are materials which we find on the Earth.
They can be changed and used by people in different ways.
▲ Look at these pictures.

sheep's fleece	a nut and bolt	a path
rocks	a jumper	metal ore
a ball of wool	a metal ingot	paving slabs

▲ Find the raw materials and fill in the flow chart below
to show the changes that can happen to them.

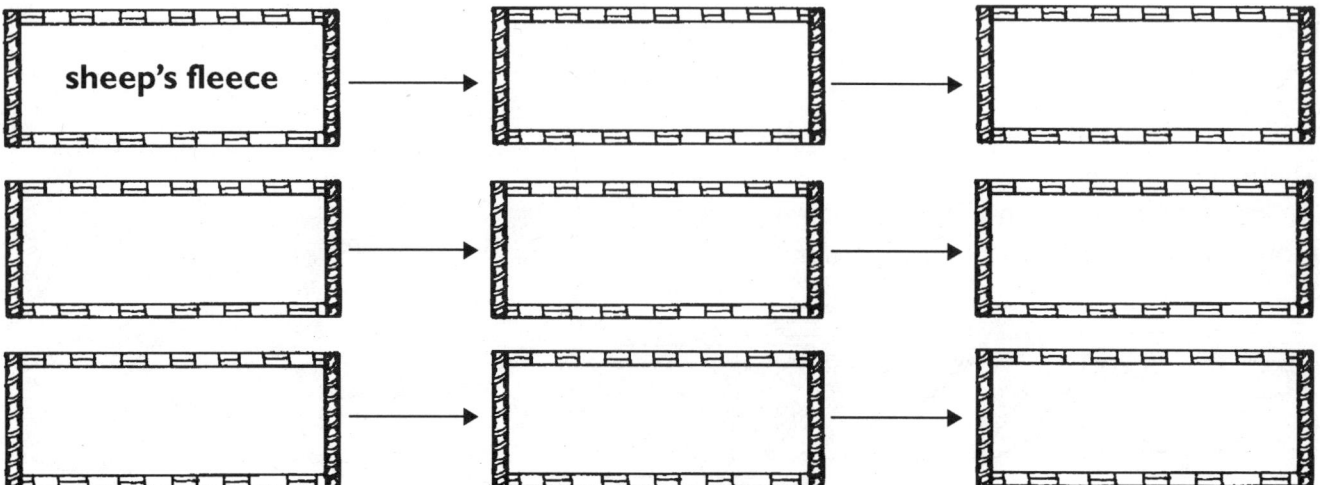

sheep's fleece	→		→	
	→		→	
	→		→	

Using the best materials for the job

You will need: a pencil; paper.

▲ Look at the pictures. Decide why each
material was used to make these objects.
Choose the two best words from those below.
You will need to use some words more than once.

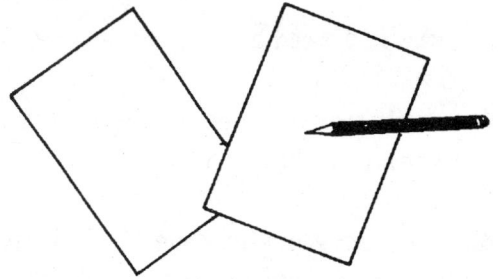

wooden door	metal bridge	plastic washing-up bowl	glass window-pane
1			
2			
plastic tube	copper wire	stone wall	wooden table
1			
2			
wooden spoon	plastic raincoat	aluminium can	woollen gloves
1			
2			

heavy	waterproof	flexible
lightweight	conducts electricity	a thermal insulator
transparent	long-lasting	attractive
strong		

▲ Choose some objects of your own.
1 Examine each one and draw it.

2 Identify the materials on your drawing.
3 Decide why they were used.

Using the Earth's materials

You will need: a red, orange (amber) and green crayon; a pencil.

▲ How do you think we should use the Earth's materials? Think carefully about each material in the table.
▲ Use the code to show how you think they should be used by choosing red, amber or green.
▲ Write down your suggestions and comments.

Colour Code

(red) Avoid using this material. Supplies are likely to run out soon.

(amber) Use this material carefully and recycle whenever possible.

(green) Although supplies seem fairly plentiful, use wisely and recycle whenever possible.

Material	Supply	Red, amber or green?	Suggestions and comments
plastic	Plastic is made from oil which will eventually run out.	◯	
metal	Metals come from under the ground. Supplies are becoming low.	◯	
hardwood	Slow-growing trees produce hardwoods. Rainforest trees are hardwood.	◯	
softwood	Coniferous trees produce softwoods. They grow fairly quickly.	◯	
natural fabrics	Some animals and plants produce natural fibres for making fabrics.	◯	
paper	Paper is made from softwood trees.	◯	
glass	A special type of sand is used for making glass.	◯	

What a waste!

You will need: a pencil.

When we have finished with things we throw
them away. Then they are buried, burned or
dumped in the sea. All these methods of
getting rid of rubbish cause pollution. It is a
good idea to try and use things over again.
We call this *recycling*.
▲ Think of all the things you throw away
every week and make a list.
▲ Which recycling container would you put
them in – A,B,C,D?

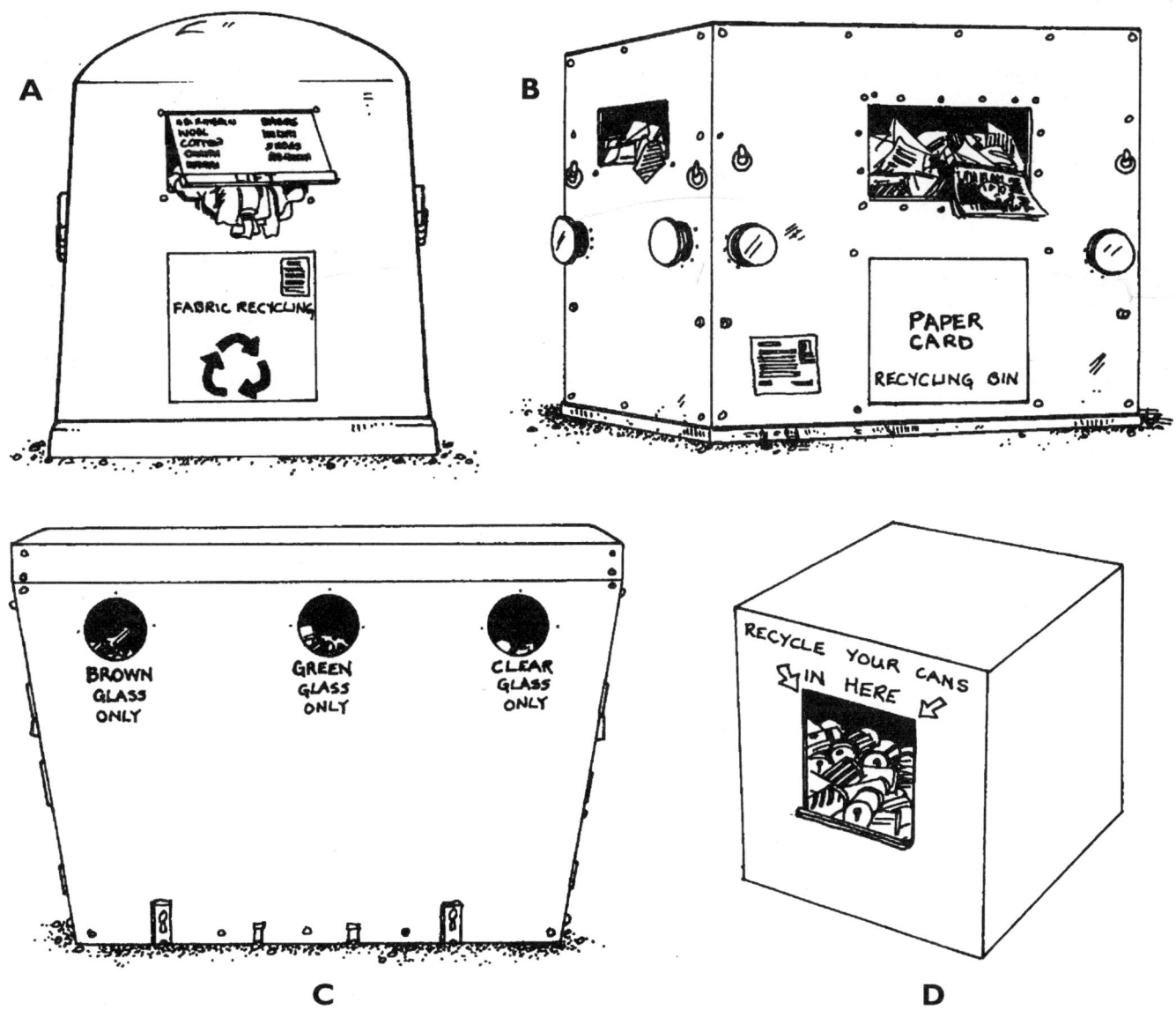

A

FABRIC RECYCLING

B

PAPER
CARD

RECYCLING BIN

C

BROWN
GLASS
ONLY

GREEN
GLASS
ONLY

CLEAR
GLASS
ONLY

D

RECYCLE YOUR CANS
IN HERE

Factories can turn these waste materials into new products.
▲ Find out where your nearest recycling points are.

Solids, liquids and gases

You will need: a pencil.

Materials can be grouped according to whether they are a solid, a liquid or a gas.

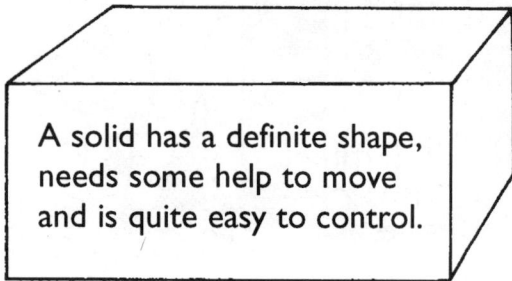

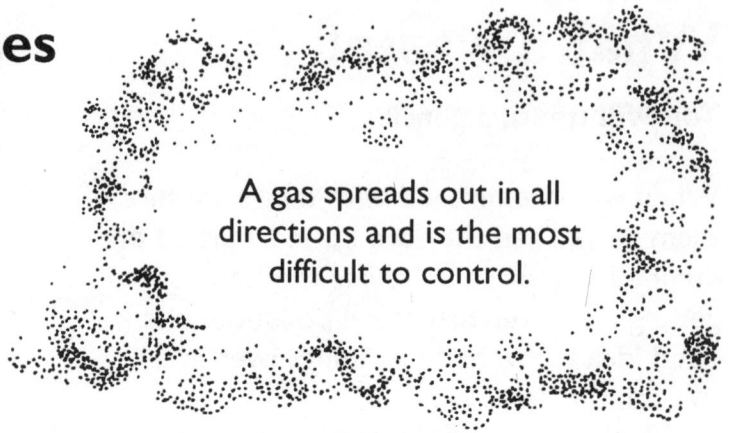

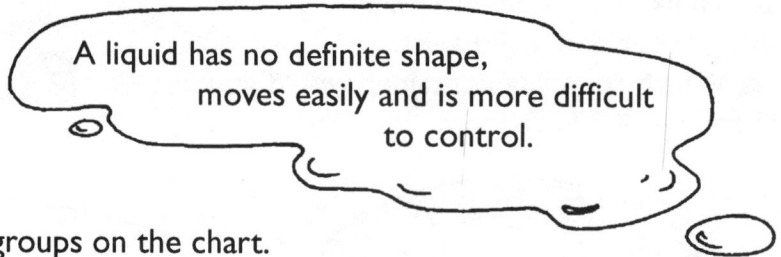

A gas spreads out in all directions and is the most difficult to control.

A solid has a definite shape, needs some help to move and is quite easy to control.

A liquid has no definite shape, moves easily and is more difficult to control.

▲ Sort these things into the correct groups on the chart.

milk	**shoe**	**car exhaust fumes**
newspaper	**engine oil**	**raindrops**
air inside a balloon	**person's breath**	**brick**

▲ Add some solids, liquids and gases of your own.

Solids	Liquids	Gases

▲ Which list is the most difficult to complete?

Looking at liquids

You will need: food colouring; a jug of water; a sheet of thin plastic; a plastic bottle with a cap; a collection of small different-shaped containers; a pencil.

Liquids do not have a shape of their own.
They take the shape of the container they are in.
▲ Put a few drops of food colouring into a jug of water. Pour the coloured water into different-shaped containers.

a test tube
a saucer
a small vase
a jar
a bun tin
a piece of plastic tube
a mug

▲ Try to draw the shapes the water makes.

▲ Fill an egg cup with coloured water.
1 Notice the shape of the water.
2 Pour the water into a saucer.
3 Notice the shape of the liquid now.
4 Carefully pour the water onto a plastic sheet.
5 Draw the shape of the water.

▲ Half-fill a plastic bottle with coloured water.
1 Fasten the cap on tightly.
2 Draw the shape of the liquid.
3 Tilt the bottle and draw the shape the liquid takes.
4 Lay the bottle on its side and draw the shape of the liquid now.

▲ Name _____

Moving liquids

You will need: a dropper or pieces of a straw; small amounts of honey, treacle, cooking oil, washing-up liquid; plastic spoons; a pencil; a box or card to make a slope; smooth paper.

▲ Watch a tap as it drips. Try to describe how the drip forms.
▲ Use a dropper or a piece of a straw to make drops of other liquids. Try using honey, treacle, cooking oil and washing-up liquid.
▲ Draw the shapes of the drops in the table.

Honey	Treacle	Cooking oil	Washing-up liquid

▲ Are the drops all the same size?
▲ Do they all form and fall in the same way?

Liquids flow downhill because of the force of gravity. Some liquids are thicker and stickier than others.

▲ Find out if all liquids flow downhill at the same rate.
1 Make a slope out of a box or card.
2 Cover the slope with smooth paper.
3 Put a spoonful of each different liquid at the top of the slope.
▲ Which liquid flowed most easily?
▲ Which liquid took the longest to reach the bottom of the slope?

Looking at gases

You will need: scissors; paper; crayons; thread.

Most gases are difficult to see. They move into spaces in all directions and are difficult to control.
▲ Look around for signs of gases.

▲ How are gases useful in each of these pictures?

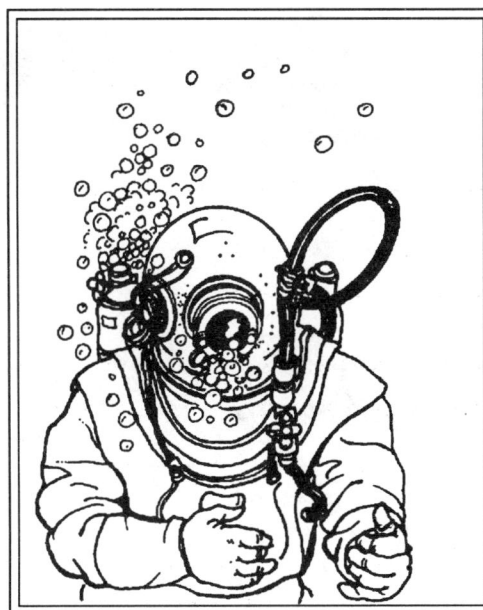

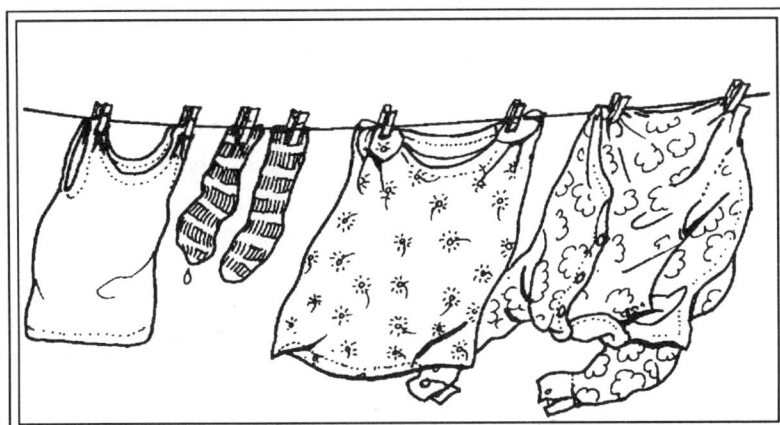

The air around us is made up of different gases:
Nitrogen   78%
Oxygen   21%
Carbon dioxide 0.03%
Other gases   0.97%

Air rises when it is warm.
▲ Make a spiral snake to hang above a radiator.
It will detect rising air.
1 Draw a spiral.
2 Colour the snake and give it an eye.
3 Cut along the line.
4 Fasten it to a piece of thread.
5 Hold it carefully over the hot radiator. What happens to the snake?

Making and collecting gases

You will need: two small plastic bottles; a balloon; bicarbonate of soda; vinegar; a teaspoon; a paper funnel; a pencil.

When some materials are mixed together, a gas is made.
▲ Try this experiment to make a gas.
1 Put a teaspoonful of bicarbonate of soda into a bottle. Use a paper funnel.
2 Carefully pour a small amount of vinegar into the bottle.
3 Put your thumb over the opening of the bottle.
▲ What do you feel? What do you see? What do you hear?

▲ Practise fitting the balloon over the neck of another bottle. You will need to be able to do this quickly.
1 Mix the bicarbonate of soda and vinegar again.
2 Put the balloon over the neck of the bottle as quickly as you can.
3 Describe what happens.
▲ Where did the gas go in the first test? Where did the gas go in the second test?

▲ Write down the names of any gases you know.

▲ Add to your collection of names as you learn more about gases.

Comparing solids, liquids and gases

You will need: a pencil.

▲ Do the words below describe a solid, a liquid or a gas? Write them on the chart in the correct spaces. Some descriptions can be used more than once.

keeps its own shape
spreads out in all directions
takes the shape of the container it is in
flows down hills
flows easily through a pipe

has no definite shape
can be squashed into a smaller volume
drips
can sometimes be used for building
is usually easy to handle

A solid	A liquid	A gas
Containers	Containers	Containers

▲ Are these containers useful for holding a solid, a liquid or a gas?

a balloon   a bottle   a straw
a schoolbag   a jar   a flask
a pair of lungs an oxygen cylinder a box
a cupboard   a hose-pipe

▲ Add their names to the table. Some containers could be useful for holding two different materials.

Identifying solids, liquids and gases

You will need: a pencil; reference books.

Solids, liquids and gases are all around us.
▲ Can you identify a solid, a liquid and a gas
that might be present in each of these pictures?

1

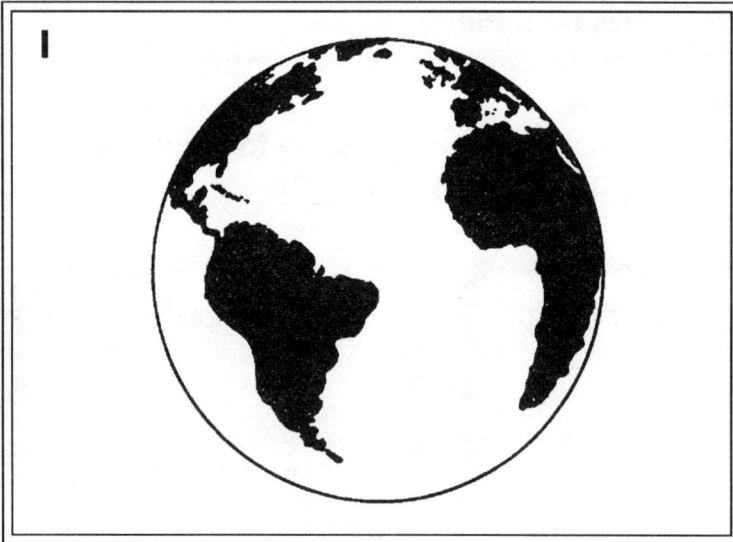

solid: _____

liquid: _____

gas: _____

2

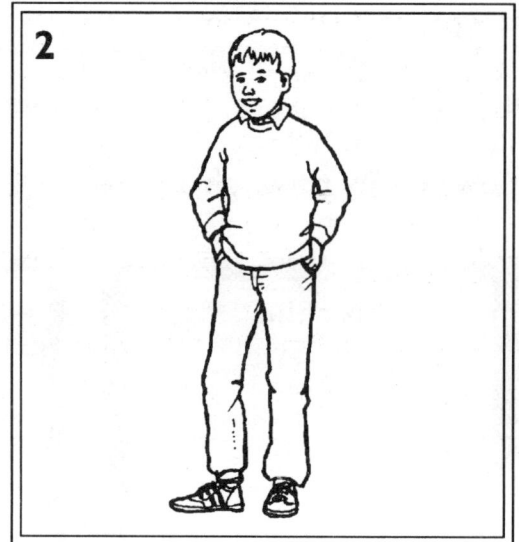

solid: _____

liquid: _____

gas: _____

3

solid: _____

liquid: _____

gas: _____

4

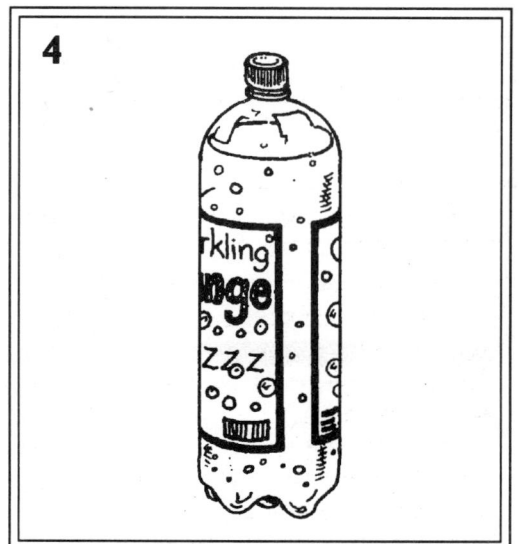

solid: _____

liquid: _____

gas: _____